GODFATHERISM VIRUS

Alex Ndukwe

First printing, 2020

Printed in the United States of America

ISBN: 9798694818001

Dedication

This Book is dedicated to Mr **Godwin Obaseki**, Governor of Edo State, he stood firm against Godfatherism, I supported him during the just concluded elections and we could see the face of our democratic values.

Forward

Our democracy is evolving, most advanced democracies in the world have had challenges and over time they have fine tunned processes and behavioural patterns associated with it.

This book discusses godfatherism, a virus that is a threat to our democratic values, without mincing words this challenge has been in our polity since first republic but the intensions are quite different from today, at that time more credence was given to ensuring that good governance was delivered to the people, the godsons were mentored by their godfathers like ZIK, AWO, TAFAWA BALEWA. The followers of these leaders are still around today, you will hear acronyms like awoist, zikist etc.

Today Godfatherism is geared towards financial gains, this would affect service delivery to the people, infrastructural deficits become the order of the day. There is no region in Nigeria that has not been affected by this virus.

A. Ndukwe

Table of Contents

Godfatherism Synopsis

Wiktionary defines Godfatherism as a form of political corruption in which an influential member of a party assists another person/party in the climb to leadership due to many reasons including unpopularity of the latter. This has been a popular phenomenon in Nigeria, when a leader completes his two terms as stipulated by the constitution, the fellow anoints a successor and in most cases cannot be a popular personality , the Godfather makes effort to introduce him/her to the people , canvasing for votes.

Godfathers are powerbrokers in Nigerian politics. People throng into and out of their houses daily, running errands or seeking one favour or another. The relationship between political godfathers and their adopted sons is usually transactional in nature: it is a case of 'you rub my back, and I rub your back', as Nigerians say. Like every businessman, godfathers invest in their 'grandsons' and expect returns after elections. This is often through juicy ministerial appointments, contracts, land allocations, sharing of political influence and power with incumbents, and if the accusations against some of them are to be taken seriously, unjustified demand for allocation of state financial resources. The favours a godfather demands and gets from his godson are for strategic reasons. In most cases, he asks for the right to nominate about eighty percent of those to serve in the cabinet of his godson.

Many godfathers also ensure that they control most of the members of state houses of assembly in Nigeria. They readily use these people to threaten the governors with impeachment any time there is a disagreement. All these strategic antics provide a godfather the effective control of the regime he helped to put in place. Should the godson prove stubborn later, the godfather can always use his nominees in the regime to intimidate him. His nominees in the regime are also another source of money-making. This enables the godfather to 'eat with both hands'. As the principal godsons bring monthly 'kola' ('ransom fees') to the godfather, those imposed as commissioners, permanent secretaries board chairmen, etc., make

similar monthly payments. At the end of the day, the godfather makes more money from the political process than any other person.

        This phenomenon is common in Africa, in Nigeria it is a part and parcel of our democracy. I have come to realize that incumbents usually anoint a successor that will take over reigns of power from them, without having any track record or any laudable achievements or experience. ensure they emerge as candidate during primary elections and subsequently presented to the people during campaign. The people would vote for them blindly since he/she represent the ruling party.

Apart from the fact that it is a faulty selection process because the fellow might not be experienced, qualified, exposed, creative in terms of bringing development to the environment which he/she would oversee. Interestingly most Nigerian leaders are beneficiary of this system, that encourages corruption, theft of public funds and underdevelopment.

Our democratic process is often abused, elections are not free and fair, rigging is the order of the day, such acts are usually executed by the God fathers, once a candidate has someone behind him, victory is assured, the mechanism that involves box snatching and replacing it with stuffed box.

The electorate has clamoured for electronic voting and unfortunately this cannot happen except the amended electoral act is signed into law, our expectation is that this should happen before 2023 polls. One question we need to ask ourselves is that how candidates emerge at the advanced democracies, we do not hear about GodFatherism, in the united states we have the electoral college, this is where such decisions are taken.

Patriotism is one important attribute that is missing in our politicians, why do they want to be in politics, is it to make a living or serve the people? This questions require an answer, why is it a do or die affair during elections, such actions trigger Godfatherism, a potential candidate would now negotiate with a high ranking and influential politician for support and a negotiation takes place, the high ranking politician comes up with a price that must be paid when success is attained, an example is Dr Chris Ngige collaborated with Chris Uba and the candidate had to take an oath at the okija shrine that he will keep to the agreement, unfortunately he defaulted. This Led to his kidnap, it is embarrassing that a governor that should be the chief security officer of his state was abducted.

Apparently, he did not compromise by using public funds to settle his Godfather, another method was used to get rid of him, he was impeached by state house of assembly. President Obasanjo described the situation, two looters could not agree on how to share the loot and therefore you have such an ugly situation in Anambra state.

Godfatherism, a virus that is worst than COVID19 has ravaged our democratic values since first republic.

Chapter 1

History of God Fatherism in Politics

The advent of godfatherism in the Nigerian partisan politics dates back to the First Republic when leaders of the three major political parties (Northern Peoples Congress (NPC), Action Group (AG) and National Congress of Nigerian Citizens (NCNC) carefully and meticulously cultivated godsons that they were convinced would advance the well-being of the citizens.

Ahmadu Bello of NPC, Nnamdi Azikiwe of the NCNC and Obafemi Awolowo of the AG were motivated to do so not to use godsons as surrogates to promote parochial interests, but to promote the developmental aspirations of the people. Unlike the present crop of political godfathers, the first-generation godfathers were essentially benevolent and progressive because they did not abuse their status as godfathers by imposing frivolous demands on their godsons as it is the case today.

Literally godfathers are seen in Nigeria to be men who have the power personally to determine both who get nominated to contest elections and who wins in a state. Those who get employed in the Bureaucracy and those who get robust postings and deployments. There is no gainsaying that godfatherism is firmly established in all the sceptre of Nigeria politics and bureaucracy. It has now come to be a guiding principle in contemporary Nigeria.

They served as a huge reservoir of wisdom and experience to be

consulted on the business of governance. Indeed, in a relative sense, the first generation godfathers were drawn by community sense of interest in seeking to influence political selection and employment into the public bureaucracy or seeking to influence the electorates to vote for some candidates of their choice. It was enough satisfaction for them that they wielded tremendous influence in the society and this inevitably generated a groundswell of goodwill and reverence for them as their views on political issues were scarcely contested in their respective regions of the Country.

Corroborating the benevolence of the first-generation godfathers, understanding the role of politics as well as the military in an evolving country., Sir, Ahmadu Bello placed his godchildren in viable institutions and the rewards to the Northern Nigeria are today self-evidence; Chief Obafemi Awolowo was godfather to a large number of today's Yoruba intelligentsia that have applied his teachings for the benefit of their region; also within the Ibo community, the late Sir Odumegwu Ojukwu, was godfather to Dr. Nnamdi Azikiwe who rose to become the first Premier of the old Eastern Region and later emerged the first President of Nigeria under the defunct parliamentary arrangement.

The first godfather-godson conflict to become public knowledge under the present political dispensation in Nigeria was the one between Governor Mala Kachallah of Borno state and Senator Ali Modu Sherriff, popularly known as 'SAS'. Mallam Kachallah chose SAS as his godfather during the 1999 gubernatorial elections in Borno state. SAS had two qualities which Kachallah could hardly pretend not be aware of. He was wealthy and influential in All Nigcria Peoples Party (formerly APP), both at local and national levels. SAS was a ma-jor financier of ANPP in Nigeria. His opinions mattered a lot to the party on all things. On this account he made Kachallah win the 1999 gubernatorial election in Borno state. He also won a seat for himself at the Senate and rode on this achievement to become senate leader of All

Nigeria Peoples Party (formerly APP). The relationship between SAS and Kachallah did not just start with the 1999 elections. The two of

had always been family friends. Kachallah was

the best man when SAS's father was married to

his mother. SAS thus addressed him as 'baba' (my

father). Politics changed all this. By 1999,

Kachallah started to accord SAS the status of a

godfather and vice versa. Kachallah

condescended to this level simply because he

wanted power which he did not have the money

to acquire. He wanted to become a state

governor though he lacked the money and

grassroots support needed for winning an

election. SAS had all that Kachallah

needed, and the two of them entered a patron-

client relationship. Kachallah had what he

wanted by winning the gubernatorial election,

but SAS hardly got what he wanted: 'profit' from

his investment.

The conflict between Kachallah and SAS

started immediately the results of the 1999

election were announced. Several factors must

have led to the problem but the most popularly

known was that Kachallah rejected the list of commissioners suggested for his cabinet by SAS and drew up an 'integrated' list consisting of those suggested by his godfather, 'Borno elders', and himself. He was opposed to a situation where SAS would have to dictate everything. The political environment of Borno state became heated as a result. This was to the extent that the last military administrator of Borno state noted before handing over to Kachallah that there were already plans to impeach him.

As predicted, Kachallah's problems became more compounded immediately he took overpower. He had to contend with a hostile House of Assembly dominated and led by other godsons of SAS. Most of those invited to serve in his cabinet were later found to be die-hard supporters of SAS as well. All these people, known in Borno politics as 'Bama mafia', soon started to attack the governor on different fronts. SAS adopted a two-pronged approach in dealing with his son. The first was to work with the state House of Assembly to get Kachallah impeached. The second is an alternative to the first: to discredit Kachallah so much that it would be impossible to be given a second term in office in 2003. Supporters of Kachallah had to fight back using political thugs known as 'ECOMOG'. The camp of SAS established its own ECOMOG as well. The opposition party in the state, PDP, which hoped to benefit from the confusion in Borno state, also established its own ECOMOG, thus turning Borno into a violent state.

Several lives were lost in the process. The Borno state House of Assembly was also set on fire by ECOMOG. As the ANPP in the state became factionalised, Kachallah went to court claiming that his own faction was the authentic one.

The court agreed. The camp of SAS challenged the court judgment and won the case. This enabled SAS to formally take over the control of ANPP in the state. Kachallah had no other option but to decamp to Alternative for

Democracy (AD). He contested the 2003
election on the platform of the party and lost.
SAS dropped his senatorial ticket and contested
the governorship position and won. This was how
SAS became the governor of Borno state.

Anambra State is one of the federating
units in Nigeria that is popularly known for
godfather politics. Between 1999 and 2003, the
fight was between Emeka Offor (Godfather and
the Governor of the State Chinwoke Mbadinuju
(godson), who refused to dance to the tune of
the godfather. This led to Mbadinuju's loosing the
gubernatorial ticket for Peoples Democratic Party
(PDP) and his subsequent inability to buy political
space in 2003. The dust raised by these to
political bigwigs was yet to settle when two other
actors emerged, Chirs Uba and Chris Ngige. Uba
was the godfather responsible for the installation
of Ngige. Ngige pledged his loyalty to Uba and
assured him of cooperation. Based on this Uba
bankrolled the generational election to the

tune of three billion naira. After the election, Ngige refused to pay back his godfather the necessary commission and patronage. And what supposed to be a cold war was made public with the abduction of Ngige and his purported resignation. Since then, peace has eluded the State until Ngige was defeated at the election petition tribunal for rigging the gubernatorial polls by the All Progressive Grand Alliance (APGA) candidate Mr. Peter Obi.

Between 1999 and 2003, the battle line in Kwara politics was well defined. Olusola Saraki, former Senate leader and political kingpin, was in contest for relevance with his former protégé, Mohamed Lawal, a retired Navy Commodore, who was the Governor of the State then. Saraki, who has installed not less than four governors in the State, including Lawal, himself, fell out with Lawal on the sharing of political booties. But Lawal did not compromise and these led to a cold war which culminated in the expulsion of Saraki from the then All People's Party (APP), now All Nigerian People's Party (ANPP) and Saraki teamed up with People's Democratic Party (PDP) in the State. Then, the 2003 elections to both men was the ultimate battle to determine the political grandmaster of the State. They deployed their vast resources to prosecute the 'war'. During this 'war' bomb blasts shattered the peace of Ilorin, this happened at the premises of National Pilot Newspaper owned by the Saraki's . Lots of people were assassinated, maimed, injured, etc. during the imbroglio.

Between 1999 and 2010, the godfather and godson battle was between Chief Jim Nwobodo and Dr. Chimaroke Nnamani. Nwobodo installed Nnamani. Nnamani could not settle Nwobodo and the two fell apart. Between 2007 and 2010 the godfather-godson battle was between former Governor Chimoroke Nnamani and Governor Sullivan Chime. Chimoroke played godfather to Chime during the 2007 gubernatorial election. He did all that were humanly possible to install Chime as the

Governor of Enugu State. As soon as Governor Chime emerged, Nnamani sent a long list of potential political appointees to Chime and demanded to remote control the leadership of the State. This did not go well with Chime and they fell headlong. Chime used his power of incumbency to outwit him and formed his government. Up till today the 'war' has not ended.

Lagos State, Tinubu is a former two-time governor of Lagos State and he retains mass support there, with crowds of people gathering outside his mansion on Bourdillon Road, Ikoyi. They credit him with the social and economic progress seen in Lagos over the past two decades. They add that he has also ensured that progressive governors run the state since he left the post. Some of Tinubu's notable achievements as governor includes improving the state's waste management system, and better incentives for civil servants (salary increases and better quality of working environments).

His successor, Babatunde Raji Fashola, was responsible for the implementation of the Bus Rapid Transit (BRT) Lite System, which ferries passengers in high-capacity buses on dedicated bus lanes. Governor Akinwunmi Ambode, the immediate past governor, was shut out when he tried to move away from Tinubu and his desires, and instead of allowing him to run on the APC ticket for a second term, he was replaced by Babajide Sanwo-Olu. Governor Sanwo-Olu, the current governor, another one of Tinubu's picks, has been praised for his handling of the COVID-19 pandemic in the country's most densely populated state.

KADUNA, EL-RUFAI claims that he ended Godfatherism, it appears to be false. How can he claim he can teach Lagos on how to end this Virus. El-Rufai has been a beneficiary of godfatherism while in PDP, an unknown fellow, he became head of Bureau of Public Enterprise

(BPE) and subsequently Minister of the Federal Capital Territory administration. In 2015, he contested the APC governorship primary with the present gubernatorial candidate of the Peoples Democratic Party (PDP), Isa Ashiru Kudan, a strong grassroots politician who enjoyed massive support of party stalwarts, the likes of Yero Makama, Hakeem Baba Ahmed, Tom Maiyashi, Tijani Ramalan Yero, Amb. Sule Buba, who are strong members of the party. Eventually, what gave el-Rufai an edge was the singular act of General Muhammadu Buhari's endorsement as the state's APC gubernatorial candidate. Buhari contested for Presidency as of then, thus making it easy for el Rufai to benefit massively from the APC bandwagon.

To add to the partiality el Rufai enjoyed, when Isa Ashiru and others ran their campaigns for their primary, Buhari did not attended their campaigns, but when el-Rufai flagged off his campaign, Buhari attended and raised his hand as his preferred candidate and that was what changed the game. Buhari raising el-Rufai's hand, Buhari made personal calls and even invitation to some party stakeholders where he personally intervened to canvass support for el-Rufai, then what do we call this.

Adams Oshiomhole and Godwin Obaseki have been in the news for a while before the elections in Edo state, the candidate he once marketed to the people of Edo state suddenly disqualified with flimsy excuses that his credentials had issues, its rather unfortunate that academicians from the ivory towers are usually used to perpetuate electoral evil in Nigeria , I was disappointed to see the drama unfold to this point. Apparently, the Godfather did not want him to run for second term. This triggered my interest to see how Obaseki will handle this issue, I carried out a research to find out if really he had been a good leader and review projects he has executed in his tenure that was about to end. It was evident that the electorate loved him, and he had done a good Job in Edo state, the party he wished to run with did not matter. I want to thank God with the outcome of the result, I am not an Edo indigene, but I monitored the results as it was been released.

There is hope that this virus will be eradicated in Nigeria, Ambode of Lagos could not wither the storm when it became clear that the Godfather of Lagos did not want him anymore, this man transformed Lagos , Pastor E.A Adeboye , General Overseer of RCCG intervened and the Godfather said his hands were tied and there is nothing he can do. Edo story will not be forgotten in the history of Nigeria's Democracy.

"In life, you work hard and leave di rest to God. You do your best and trust God to bless your hustle. I feel good, I feel healthy, I feel strong, thank God. For life, you win some and you lose some, but life goes on."

('Adams Oshiomhole react to Godwin Obaseki Edo state victory', BBC, September 24, 2020)

The Godfather accepting the outcome in good faith, I am pleased with this development, the polls were free and fair , the people rose to the occasion.

This virus is worst than covid19, apart from its adverse effects on our polity, it has also ravaged our public institutions making them feeble and weak, deliveries cannot get to the people.

'The acting Managing Director of the Niger Delta Development Commission (NDDC), Kemebradikumo Pondei, has management and staff the commission spent N1.5 billion on themselves to cushion the impact of COVID-19 on their lives.'

('COVID-19: We Used N1.5bn To Care For Ourselves – NDDC MD', The interview Magazine, July 7 2020)

Let me give an example NDDC, to my knowledge is the richest public institution in Nigeria, the question which I would love us to ponder on is how do they appoint Managing Director of this Agency? Its purely a Godfather somewhere ensures he puts someone that would be loyal.

"I pity Professor Pondei. He looks to me like a gentleman but he couldn't hold his ground. Akpabio told me, as he did to my predecessor, Mrs. Akwagaga, to change all the Dollars ($120,000,000) in the account of the NDDC at the time to pay for his contracts, the desilting contracts that he got, the water hyacinth and all. Mrs. Akwagaga got afraid and ran to the Chairmen of the National Assembly Committees on NDDC, and they now gave her cover. Akpabio offered to give the NDDC Committee Chairmen N400 million cash, if they can tell this woman (Mrs. Akwagaga) that they should change $120 million in the NDDC account and let him have access so that he would be able to use

the funds to take care of certain people in Nigeria. They now promised to get back to him. To cover the woman, they now wrote to her that she is not allowed to change one dollar in the account. That letter from the Committee chairmen protected the woman and Akpabio was bitter with her and similarly started attacking the Committee Chairmen in the National Assembly.'

('Controversy! As Akpabio, Nunieh street fight gets messier' , Bussinesday, Jul 19 2020, Ignatius Chukwu)

Can we see what godfatherism has turned our public institution to, Akpabio instructing that monies be changed from dollars to Naira, making promise to the members of National assembly, what a shame on us as a country, what corruption are we fighting if a pubic officer would promise lawmakers a gift in a bid to achieve his ulterior motives.

I also find it difficult to understand why contracts would be awarded to members of National assembly and the projects would not be executed, the same Lawmakers are to investigate NDDC, what kind of drama is this. I wonder why EFCC has not done anything with respect to this matter.

Chapter 2

Effects on our society

The effects of godfatherism is enormous and we intend to discuss it extensively, they are as follows:

a) **Underdevelopment**
b) **Triggers Poor Economy**
c) **Poor Democratic Values**
d) **Weak Public Institutions**
e) **Promotes Corruption**

These are the main effects of this virus on our nation, interestingly the decay has existed for a long time and I can recall a former Head of state boasting on the number of people he had made billionaires in Nigeria, this is rather unfortunate and painful to hear an elder states man make such comments. Unfortunately, it has been in existence for long and responsible for Africa been the poorest continent. Though our focus is on Nigeria.

Underdevelopment

Nigeria's huge infrastructural deficit remains a topical discourse and poses a major hindrance to the growth of businesses and economic prosperity. From poor port infrastructure, dilapidated transport networks, epileptic power supply, huge housing deficit, Nigeria's infrastructure gap cannot be overemphasized. Recently, the Minister of Finance stated Nigeria needs an estimated N36tn annually for the next 30 years to solve Nigeria's infrastructure problem. Clearly, the sum spent by the government annually on capital projects is significantly short of the sum needed to tackle Nigeria's infrastructure problems.

In our view, the core reason behind the government's inability to spend adequately on infrastructure is down to the

government's tight fiscal position. Thus, we see need for the government to actively implement fiscal consolidation measures which would include driving revenue earning initiatives as well as blocking revenue slippages. However, we believe the need to involve the private sector through public-private partnerships remains Nigeria's best option to tackle its widening infrastructure gap.
(Nigeria's Infrastructure Gap; Too Little Too Late? Proshare, November 15, 2019)

The virus had cumulative effects with respect to infrastructural Gap, a newly installed government is not allowed to carryout promises made to the electorate, it would now be the time to make returns, the funds that would have been used to execute projects would flow into pockets of individuals. Corruption is an appendage of godfatherism, this phenomenon has been in existence for a long time. Though I agree some school of thoughts would argue that Afterall we have been in military rule for over 30 years, I quite agree but the virus was also in existence at that time. All these governments put together is responsible for our predicament today.

"Make hay while the sun shines.", an idiomatic expression dating back to Medieval times, we experienced boom in the early seventies, during the gulf war of 1993, we have enjoyed excess earnings from our crude sales but the virus would not allow us deploy these earnings accurately in improving or upgrading infrastructures , better still research into new technologies. The opportunities are lost now, this is responsible for the pain the government are going through today. Monies must be borrowed to execute projects, I explained to my friends complaining that Nigeria is borrowing so much now. Constructing a 4th mainland bridge of 2nd Niger bridge today would cost a fortune compared to what it would have been if it was done in 1993 during the excess crude oil earning days, it would have been very convenient because the funds are available then. At every point of our history the virus had existed, public institutions were flooded with godsons and they had no choice but to be loyal to their benefactors.

What roles are the egg heads playing in the quest to improve technologies, rather than been used as puppets by the godfathers to disqualify credible candidates during primary elections. Power is another infrastructure that is underdeveloped, today we still use pump hydro and thermal plants for energy generation on our national Grid, we continue to celebrate mediocrity and collapse of our national grid. The policy makers would have taking a cue from the renewable energy technology as a means of improving our power supply nationwide. Resources would be required for this laudable research, but the virus has taken it away. Without adequate power we cannot have an industrial revolution, most manufacturing firms have moved their plants to Ghana, because of stable electricity.

Unfortunately, our nation would have been more developed than the Asian Tigers, we cannot give up now, orientation must change, our patriotic values must improve. Our democracy is evolving, we must solve this problem permanently to ensure that we do not put huge debt burdens on generations unborn.

Triggers Poor Economy

When there is underdevelopment it affects the economy adversely, the refineries in Nigeria are not working up to its installed capacity, products can only be imported. Subsidy must be removed because of the effects of Covid19 and the government cannot afford this expense. Pump price of petroleum products was marginally increased, this would technically increase the prices of commodities. Let us look at the refineries, an Infrastructure poorly managed by NNPC, another weak public institution that has never lived to expectation.

'The four refineries were completed between 1965 and 1989 and have a combined capacity of 445,000bl/d, which should be sufficient to meet around 70pc of daily domestic demand. The quartet registered combined operational expenses of NGN142.1bn ($367mn) in the 12 months to 30 June despite being out of service, according to the country's NOC, Nigerian National Petroleum Corporation (NNPC).'

These refineries do not have control over crude purchase of crude, storage and marketing of products, another subsidiary of NNPC handles this function. Refineries in Nigeria are not running as a firm and this led to their collapse. Turnaround maintenance are not properly executed for so many years, though I quite agree that NNPC has lots of structures aimed at managing these refineries but unfortunately corruption had existed over the years, still affects this installed infrastructure today. The Dangote refinery is still been constructed and when its operational could ease the pain, but the government owned should be revamped as well for a healthy competition that would also aid the price war ahead. Professionalism have been compromised with reference to discussions in this book, it is unbelievable that refineries cannot work optimally for the last 3 decades, it calls for a sober reflection, obviously some things are not correct, public institutions like NNPC should not be a father Christmas but a business entity that should be ran for profit and not a conduit pipe for corruption. These institutions must be privatised so that government would remove its hands from its operation. How can we attract foreign investors if our economy is poor , it's absolutely difficult.

Poor Democratic Values

I want to specifically thank the Lord with the outcome of the just   concluded elections in Edo, even PMB acknowledged that the wishes of the people was not thwarted and thus we have ray of hope that our democratic dispensation would definitely improve someday. In my book on 'e-voting can be a success' I mentioned the 'Democracy index' , compiled by the Economist Intelligence Unit (EIU), a UK-based company. It intends to measure the state of democracy in 167 countries, of which 166 are sovereign states and 164 are UN member states. based on 60 indicators grouped in five different categories, measuring pluralism, civil liberties, and political culture. In addition to a numeric score and a ranking, the index categorises each country into one of four regime types: **full democracies**, **flawed democracies**, **hybrid regimes** and **authoritarian regimes**.

Let us not digress from our focus, Godfatherism has effects on our democratic values, it triggers rigging of elections, ballot box snatching, credibility of the polls are suspect, electorate refusing to participate, Violence etc. The Godfather has marketed his candidate and would ensure that the said candidate wins the election. This leads to rigging of the election and this affects our index. Afterwards the elected officer would struggle considering demands from the King maker, this makes the people to lose confidence in the system. The number of registered voters is not equivalent to votes cast; many would avoid been part of a system that is not transparent.

Electronic voting would improve the process of voting to a larger extent but there is need for the electoral reform bill to be signed into law, before INEC can introduce it, this would definitely improve credibility of the outcomes of an election.

Nigeria is ranked 109 on the democracy index, calssified as a hybrid regime, nation with regular electoral frauds, preventing them from being fair and free democracies. These nations commonly have governments that apply pressure on political opposition, non-independent judiciaries, widespread corruption, harassment and pressure placed on the media, anaemic rule of law, and more pronounced faults than flawed democracies in the realms of underdeveloped political culture, low levels of participation in politics, and issues in the functioning of governance. This can improve , its all in our hands as citizens of Nigeria.

Weak Public Institutions

Godfathers would submit list of those he wants to be appointed into newly constituted cabinet of his godson, the effects is that less qualified candidates are involved, this transcends to the institutions as well. Our institutions become weak, corrupt because someone must receive returns. The rots continue and this affects our economy, poor service delivery, accountability etc. I have given an example with the state of our refineries managed by NNPC. I recall the substantive claims made by former CBN Governor, Lamido Sanusi on the missing 20 billion Dollars during Goodluck Jonathan's Government.

'Sanusi's letter and documents do not state whether he thinks the money was stolen or lost through mismanagement. Nor did he make allegations of illegal acts against any specific individuals or entities. Both corruption and bad

governance are perennial problems in Africa's most populous nation, and central issues in elections due on Feb. 14. Nigeria's oil industry accounts for around 95 percent of the country's foreign exchange earnings. If Nigeria continued to leak cash at the rate described in his letter to the president, Sanusi said at the time, the consequences for the economy would be disastrous. Specifically, the failure of state-owned Nigerian National Petroleum Corporation "to remit foreign exchange to the Federation Account in a period of rising oil prices has made our management of exchange rates and price stability ... extremely difficult," he wrote.'

Lack of accountability by NNPC , which the government considered an embarrassment for CBN governor to speak in the media, the virus is in operation, monies are not remitted to Federation account, an evidence of weak public institution, a product of godfatherism. In most advanced countries the minister of petroleum would have resigned but that is not the practice in Africa.

Promotes Corruption

These godfathers are not mere financiers of political campaigns. Rather they are individuals whose power stems not just from wealth but from their ability to deploy violence and corruption to manipulate national, state or local political systems in support of the politicians they sponsor. In return, they demand a substantial degree of control over the governments they help bring into being—not in order to shape government policy, but to exact direct financial "returns" in the form of government resources stolen by their protégés or lucrative government contracts awarded to them as further opportunities for graft. Godfathers also require their sponsored politicians to use government institutions to generate patronage for other protégés.

Former Oyo State governor Victor Olunloyo explained the relationship between politicians and their "godfathers" this way: Money flows up and down…these honorable members [of the Oyo State House of Assembly], during the election period, they want the patronage of the puppeteer. Afterwards money will flow in the opposite direction—back from the puppet to the puppeteer.

(Human Rights Watch interview with Victor Olunloyo, Ibadan, February 8, 2007.)

Godfatherism is both a symptom and a cause of the violence and corruption that together permeate the political process in Nigeria. Public officials who owe their position to the efforts of a political godfather incur a debt that they are expected to repay without end throughout their tenure in office. Godfathers are only relevant because politicians can deploy violence and corruption with impunity to compete for office in contests that often effectively, and sometimes actually, exclude

Nigeria's voters altogether. But their activities also help to reinforce the central role of violence and corruption in politics by making it even more difficult to win elected office without resorting to the illegal tactics they represent. Nigeria's godfatherism phenomenon is not unique to the ruling PDP, but as with many of the other abuses described in this report it is seen most often in the conduct of PDP officials as both a cause and a result of the party's success in maintaining itself in power.

There is a direct relationship between corruption and political violence—many public officials use stolen public revenues to pay for political violence in support of their ambitions. As one Niger Delta academic who maintains that his 2003 Senate campaign was derailed by the violent efforts of the PDP to intimidate voters and rig the vote, "Most of these politicians are linked to cult groups—they finance them, they maintain them, they sustain them. And all of this is out of the use of government funds." In Gombe State, a leading lawyer and former minister in the federal government published allegations in the national press that the state government was funding the activities of "Kalare" thugs using public money.

The money that is poured into mobilizing political violence in Nigeria is substantial, even if the amounts that filter down to low level thugs sometimes are not. As one civil society leader in Katsina State explained to Human Rights Watch, "They [local politicians] will just come and gather the youth to cause mayhem—not even for N5000, just N1000 or 500. To someone who is doing nothing, N50 can be something to him." Or as one former cult member in Port Harcourt put it: "The youth have no money—if you show them the bag of money or the bag of guns, they will work for you."

The amounts paid to violent actors become less trivial higher up in the chain of command or for more important operations. One engineering graduate student in Anambra State revealed that he had been paid N25,000 by the campaign office of PDP gubernatorial candidate Andy Uba to help organize thugs that chased elected delegates away from polling areas on the day of the PDP gubernatorial primaries in late 2006. He said that he was bused to the voting centers along with at least two to three busloads full of other cult and gang members who received the same payment. As of then, N25,000 was more than three times the starting monthly wage of many civil servants in Anambra State.

Chapter 3

Eradicating the virus called God Fatherism

Primary elections are internal party processes that choose a political party's candidate(s) for the next general election by holding an internal election. Exactly how this is done depends on the legal framework, internal party rules, and informal practices. Primary elections are an example of a selection process with a high level of participation, meaning that ordinary members (or in some cases all voters in the electoral district) control the process.

(Rose, Gavin M. Taking the Initiative: Political Parties, Primary Elections, and the Constitutional Guarantee of Republican Governance. Indiana University School of Law (Indiana Law Journal, vol. 81, No. 2, April 2006). And Salih, M. A. Mohamed (et al). Political Parties in Africa: Challenges for Sustained Multiparty Democracy.)

Every stakeholder must play his role effectively to eradicate this virus, we must be willing to be patriotic at all levels. Another issue is the robustness of our political parties and I would like to challenge our political class, 'Do we really have political parties or merely association pretending to be a political party?', the Framework for selecting a consensus candidate is usually abused, an incumbent Leader picks someone of his choice as his preferred candidate and at the end of the day, credible candidates must step down. The Godfather would convince the other candidates, most times they are induced with monitory rewards.

Prospective candidates must resist this kind of moves, the political parties must be active in this direction, INEC should ensure compliance as the umpire, Political parties should reject anointed candidates.

The Political parties must live up to expectation in this regard, the need to look at existing framework on candidate selection, I quite agree that parameters like popularity, strength, experience are very important trait when deciding who can be a flagbearer, its better to discontinue such and allow a level playing ground for anyone interested to contest, though it is a difficult

Age groups	Both sexes	Males	Females
0–4	22,594,967	11,569,218	11,025,749
5–9	20,005,380	10,388,611	9,616,769
10–14	16,135,950	8,504,319	7,631,631
15–19	14,899,419	7,536,532	7,362,887
20–24	13,435,079	6,237,549	7,197,530
25–29	12,211,426	5,534,458	6,676,968
30–34	9,467,538	4,505,186	4,962,352
35–39	7,331,755	3,661,133	3,670,622

40–44	6,456,470	3,395,489	3,060,981
45–49	4,591,293	2,561,526	2,029,767
50–54	4,249,219	2,363,937	1,885,282
55–59	2,066,247	1,189,770	876,477
60–64	2,450,286	1,363,219	1,087,067
65–69	1,151,048	628,436	522,612
70–74	1,330,597	765,988	564,609
75–79	579,838	327,416	252,422
80–84	760,053	408,680	351,373
85+	715,226	404,021	311,204
Total	140,431,790	71,345,488	69,086,302

Distribution of population by age groups and sex, Nigeria 2006

task but we must defend our democracy, an incumbent has the tendency to influence the party, inducing the principals of the party with money and he can have his way and the party adopts him as their sole candidate , this same fellow will one day bring a candidate of his choice, this rubbish must be discontinued.

We need a revolution, without shedding any blood or allowing any kind of violence, it is expedient for the youths to rise to the challenge.

This Table is the population of Nigeria with respect to age distribution as at 2006, the population is about 140million , the Age group 20-64 has a total of 62.1 million , which accounts for 44.3% of the population , these are the game changers, if these ones can be patriotic and become more active in our democracy.

we have depended so much on recycled leaders and the time has come for the youths of this country to wake up and be involved, the future is in their hands. Yakubu Gowon became military head of state at the age of 31, this can happen once more, the youths have to displace the old brigade, they have plundered our nation and thrown us into poverty with their recklessness and corruption. There will be no shedding of blood, but we must be interested in project Nigeria and be actively involved. It would be a taboo to have a PVC and refuse to participate in elections, our votes is enough to remove bad leaders. This age bracket we have professionals, we need to rescue Nigeria from the hands of these illiterates that do not know their left from right immediately. The revolution in Ethiopia was spear headed by a girl of 24 years, 'They wanted Al-Bashir to resign after ruling for 30 years', they got their demands. The time has come for the youths of Nigeria to rise, we cannot have Godfatherism in our polity, if we are actively involved.

The umpire INEC would look at the purported reforms and push for its amendments to include the following:

a) Reduce the multiparty system to two political parties, like practiced during June 12 polls, SDP, and NRC, we can adopt APC and PDP, the others should be deregistered.

b) Electronic voting should be implemented as soon as possible, I'm pleased to see INEC entertaining some suppliers of Voting machines, my book on 'E-voting can be a success in Nigeria', this book recommended EVM made in India , it has been in use since 1982, it cannot be manipulated, hacked or compromised. It is a standalone machine that runs on finger batteries, this implies that implementing at the rural areas without electricity would be hitch free. INEC should appreciate the fact that E-Voting failed in Germany, an advanced democracy. With the technology that suits our environment, we can organise a credible election, this would make more people involved, turnaround time and consequently our democratic index would improve.

c) The Government of the day is interested in good democratic values, without mincing words, the Edo election proved this point, Mr president and the Leadership of his party congratulated the opposition party for their victory. I was excited with this development, though INEC and Police got the credit, I believe the Edo people should be praised for not allowing their state to be hijacked by the God Father. Our Process must be modified and improved, the card reader has always given us problems, replacing this technology would cost us a fortune but we need to look for how to improve this service, except the new EVM would have an authenticity module before the vote is cast. Our processes must be simple for the electorate.

d) Would like to reiterate that our youths should refuse been used by politicians to perpetuate violence during an election, no matter the financial inducement, please resist and remember that no one is greater than our country Nigeria.

e) The political party have a lot of work with respect to choosing a candidate that would run for election. Party primaries have been abused, the party should provide a level playing ground for prospective candidates, most times processes is not devoid of money politics, contestants are settled with huge sum of money for them to step down and adopt a particular candidate. Henceforth its advisable to allow the people choose whom their flagbearer should be, we need to be wary of this and this is a fallout of Godfatherism, should be discouraged. The entire world is watching us and making a jest of our democracy.

f) Incumbent Leader about to complete their tenure should desist from anointing a successor, there many reasons such happens and its in a bid to cover his/her corrupt practices, create juicy contracts while out of office. The Lagos state Godfather is a classical example, his firm was awarded the contract to collect tax on behalf of Lagos state and 10% of the collection goes to his firm. This made it paramount for him to decide who will be governor to protect the interest of this firm that belongs to him. The same firm tried collecting tax for other state government, I recall Kano state government disengaged them some years ago considering the cost of service. The Lagos story is quite pathetic, Ambode could not run for the second term because he did not give preference to the Godfather, looking at his achievements he deserves a second term. It is pathetic that a former governor that his tenure ended in 2003 is in control of that state till now. The people can sack this godfather if they can wake up. The case of Edo should teach us a lesson. Another pretence is the continuation of programmes initiated by previous administration, this should not be the case, no matter who becomes the next leader would have to continue with existing projects. Political parties should ensure they discourage 'anointed candidate syndrome'

The stakeholders must play their roles for a lasting solution, the youths should rise to the challenge rather than complaining about poor leadership and inflicted poverty on our nation. We need to checkmate the old brigade politician, let us forget the poor performance of some youths in elected office, this should not be a yard stick for the anticipated desire that we seek. In advanced countries Youths are at the helms of affairs, this can happen in Nigeria too.

Conclusion

Godfatherism is a threat to our democracy, we have made attempts to adopt American system of governance. We need to develop home grown democratic system that would suit us, ensuring it is made less attractive and cost of governance reduced. This attributes to reasons why elections are a do or die affair, it is no longer about service to the people but a means of ensuring that the meal tickets is guaranteed.

Politics is not a vocation but service to the people, today it has become a means of livelihood, our orientation must change, this is the major reason why we cannot fight corruption as a nation. Godfatherism is a product of desperation from former office holders to continue to loot our treasuries through their installed godson. It has become a norm for some governors to collect huge pensions from the state government, continue to pursue Juicy contracts via their godson.

Though we have heard the call for restructuring from the politicians, it is just for their selfish interest and nothing more, there is no iota of patriotism in their disposition on this matter. It is all about their gains.

At this point threats to our democracy like godfatherism should be discouraged and all the stakeholders must be involved.